Edward Said and the Writing of History

Shelley Walia

Series editor: Richard Appignanesi

ICON BOOKS UK

TOTEM BOOKS USA

Published in the UK in 2001
by Icon Books Ltd., Grange Road,
Duxford, Cambridge CB2 4QF
E-mail: info@iconbooks.co.uk
www.iconbooks.co.uk

Published in the USA in 2001
by Totem Books
Inquiries to: Icon Books Ltd.,
Grange Road, Duxford,
Cambridge CB2 4QF, UK

Sold in the UK, Europe, South Africa
and Asia by Faber and Faber Ltd.,
3 Queen Square, London WC1N 3AU
or their agents

Distributed to the trade in the USA by
National Book Network Inc.,
4720 Boston Way, Lanham,
Maryland 20706

Distributed in the UK, Europe,
South Africa and Asia by
Macmillan Distribution Ltd.,
Houndmills, Basingstoke RG21 6XS

Distributed in Canada by
Penguin Books Canada,
10 Alcorn Avenue, Suite 300,
Toronto, Ontario M4V 3B2

Published in Australia in 2001
by Allen & Unwin Pty. Ltd.,
83 Alexander Street,
Crows Nest, NSW 2065

Text copyright © 2001 Shelley Walia

The author has asserted his moral rights.

Series editor: Richard Appignanesi

ISBN 1 84046 270 1

Typesetting by Wayzgoose

Printed and bound in the UK by
Cox & Wyman Ltd., Reading

Life of an Exile

The intellectual journeys of Edward W. Said, a leading literary critic and a forthright spokesman of human rights, have taken him around the world and across many disciplines, contributing substantially to the shaping of contemporary debates on Orientalism, discourse* analysis, dissident politics and postcolonialism. Examining powerful establishments of the world, Said has rendered explicit some of the key issues concerning imperialism,* under-development and culture. Taking the entire world as his home, he looks at adversial cultures and the role of the intellectual in liberating human scholarship and validating cultural forms through the reinterpretation of history. Said's critical rethinking of history is of immense significance, coming as it does in the wake of a powerful and diverse body of responses to a period of global restructuring in which insidious imperialist forces continue to influence world politics and culture.

Born in Palestine, a refugee in Egypt after the loss of Palestine in 1947, and then a migrant to the United States, Said has spent most of his life as an

* For an explanation of 'discourse' and other starred terms, see 'Key Ideas' at the end of this book.

exile from his homeland, having a deep sense of belonging to a dispossessed culture. Living under a deluge of racist outrage in the US, with right-wing conservative Americans burning down his office, Said has learnt to cope with opposition and write on the prevailing atmosphere of injustice. In a recent memoir, *Out of Place*, Edward Said traces his ambivalent and contradictory location with an increasing sense of being an outsider – a Palestinian Christian, with an English name attached to an Arabic surname, residing in America.

It was during his growing years as a student in the United States that Said gradually began to feel alienated from the pro-Israeli American culture. With the defeat of the Arabs by the Israelis in the 1967 war, the rest of Palestine was also lost and this spurred Said to think and write extensively on the Palestinian problem. In 1977, he joined the Palestine National Council, which was the parliament in exile. Ever since, he has 'tried in a certain sense, to combine [his] own literary, philosophical and cultural interests with contemporary political interests'.[1] Said's work is an endeavour to bridge the gap between the private and the public. His literary criticism is always in consonance with his personal political experience and his deeply radical and

4

oppositional stance that 'tries to speak the truth to power'.[2]

The story of Said's life is a record of an essentially lost or forgotten world. It is narrated against the background of the Second World War and Middle East politics right up until the Oslo Accord of 1993 which witnessed the compromise of Palestine. But more than these historic events, it is the story of 'the displaced form of departures, arrivals, farewells, exile, nostalgia, homesickness, belonging, and travel itself.'[3] 'The overall sensation', Said writes, 'was of always being out of place.'[4] This explains Said's 'hybridity' or the 'in-between space' that he occupies as an exile, living at the borders of inter-cultural identity. Said sees this position as one of advantage from where he can speak and write subversively, because for him the intellectual is always an 'exile or marginal'.[5]

Said feels a deep affinity with Joseph Conrad, whose homelessness finds a parallel with his own experience of being in the 'third space', almost outside in the establishment. Like Conrad, he uses his writing as a means of preventing personal disintegration – the consciousness of being an exile becomes the inspiration behind his continuing exploration of literature and politics. The end result is the exile at war with the 'real' world, the migrant sensibility struggling to find accommodation and alterations. Said's project becomes one of liberation from the official versions of history and 'truth' by building an awareness of the 'subterranean histories' which contain the real truth that is often suppressed.[6]

The Intellectual and the Politics of Location

By 1968, after the formation of the Palestine Liberation Organisation, Said had firmly resolved not to separate the personal from the political. Time had come to 'rub culture's nose in the mud of politics'.[7] The outcome of this decision was to write a dissident and subversive account of Western representations of the East.

The 1970s saw the infiltration of French high theory into the Anglo-Saxon world. It is within this context that postcolonial* cultural studies becomes institutionalised. This project, which received its initial impetus from Frantz Fanon and Aimé Cesaire, was reinforced by Edward Said in his path-breaking book *Orientalism* (1978), in which – like other Western Marxists – he emphasises the importance of culture and philosophy within Gramscian and Foucauldian paradigms of strategies of power.[8]

6

The enormity of the task of renewal within the context of a transnational economy and the collapse of socialist projects, and particularly the proclamations of the Western bourgeois school of thought dominated by Francis Fukuyama and the 'End of History' syndrome, poses problems for Said. The rigour of Said's work explores critical issues of cultural representation by unfolding epistemological shifts that have taken place under the sway of colonialism,* Orientalism, nationalism and xenophobia. His major works can be discussed in this context by arguing out his position as an intellectual who questions history, culture and literature as systems of thinking that represent images of their own creation for reasons of maintaining hegemonic structures of knowledge and power. The role of the intellectual and the relevance of the issues of culture and identity stand behind his unabashed commitment to an ideology of historical reconstruction by critical and political involvement.

In his Reith Lectures on the BBC in 1993, Said defines the intellectual as a responsible and 'oppositional' citizen who always tries to put his views outside the domain of dogmas and rigid party positions. Unlike Jean-Paul Sartre's negative intellectual who very conveniently converts a concrete situation into an abstraction, Said takes active political positions in his critical writings. These are locations which indicate how he sees the importance of critical consciousness in intellectual work. His is the 'contrapuntal' approach inherent in the sensibilities of an exile or 'the new migrant' who always believes that the power of 'the playful imagination [is] … to change forever our perception of how things are.'[9] This may be called the 'intifida of the imagination – a holy war' against the established order created by the powers that be.[10] Said's interventionist academic politics contest the strategies of establishing 'truth' through an active and involved decoding and recoding of all values, forms and histories related to the colonial project.

Said uses his position as an exile to advantage because he can raise himself above the functionless jargon and cowardice of academic intellectuals who refuse to support ideological issues in which a commitment is called for. The tensions and contradictions present in his writings – which seem to obsess critics like Ernest Gellner and Aijaz Ahmad – are the fundamental ingredients of a critic who is located ambivalently in the realms of both his professional exigencies and his public involvement, his transnational theoretical framework and his status

Said's work thus moves from literature to history and politics, and from sociology to opera and the arts. This book sets out to examine the writing of history in terms of these cultural practices and their relation to power. This makes it imperative for us to locate Said's writings within the areas of cultural and historical studies so that the deep-seated connections between history and postmodernism may be traced. The revisionist aspect of this exercise will inevitably lead to the interrogation of the transcendent reality that exists behind historical accounts.

Said has often been blamed for engaging in almost a ritual of accommodation and assimilation that does not allow him to be at home in any one culture or, for that matter, a single theoretical position. Being geographically dislocated, he has tried to negotiate his position in the context of globalisation, yet he has disrupted inter-cultural hegemony* by taking an antagonist stance against any reconciliation with Western hegemonic positions and the production of knowledge. He is, on the one hand, aware of cultural conflict and, on the other, a defender of hybridity, urging the rejection of the 'rhetoric of blame'.[12] While he understands that powerful representations do get naturally accepted, his writings argue that their inherent stereotypical nature be countered by an alternative discourse which is always conscious of the strategies of power.

The question of being an exile is inextricably linked to border-crossing and immigration which have been characteristic experiences of the twentieth century. And what better example of a migrant than Said? The location of the exile may be taken in its commonplace meaning which suggests the homelessness of the Armenians or the Jews or the Palestinians. The other exile is the intellectual who has to exile himself from what has been given to him, 'what is customary, and to see it from a point of view that looks at it as if it were something that is provisional and foreign to oneself.'[13] This second type of exile has, therefore, the connotations of independence and non-alignment, possessing the inherent qualities of both 'commitment' and 'detachment'.[14] As a committed cultural critic belonging to the world that he inhabits and the one that he has left behind, Said believes in 'things of this world' where 'human beings make their own history'.[15] This is the political recuperation, not a complete recovery, of a pristine past. It is the construction of a new world based on secular principles and justice. Like Stephen Dedalus, Said is a product of a colonial environment and 'must develop a resistant consciousness' for the affirmation of intellectual freedom.[16]

History and Postmodernism

The status of the exile itself is directly related to the emancipatory potential inherent in the task of rewriting history. We now stand at a juncture where the discipline of history is surrounded by confusion as the traditional analytical and conceptual Enlightenment structures of historical knowledge stand eroded. It is not possible ever to reconstruct the past in all its actuality, as all reconstructions are provisional and dependent on multiple interpretations. Facts no longer speak for themselves. The epistemological notions of the positivists are being challenged on the ground that history is a literary artefact and that all historical sources are intertextual.

The intrusion of politics and theory into the discipline has led to the historian becoming more and more defensive. His approach to language and the narrative conventions he has always followed is turning out to be a grossly untheorised position. It will be argued here that the possibility of destabilising the univocal and monologic historical accounts is an enabling factor in decolonisation struggles where there is an urgent need for other histories to be written and the existing to be brought under stiff scrutiny. Postmodernism undoubtedly brings a significant development to the discipline of history when looked at from a postcolonial perspective.

The catalyst for history writing came with Michel Foucault, Roland Barthes and Jacques Derrida who questioned the links between truth and the power systems which shape and determine it. They questioned the indefinite and multiplex relationship between the signifier and the signified, or, in other words, the nebulous quality of language. Language itself shapes and predetermines reality. Thus everything is a linguistic/textual construction. This debate was then taken up by Hayden White who regarded all history as verbal fiction that is partly invented. According to him, history is the persuasive composition of a point of view through the use of language. This makes it possible for us to say that historical truth is not inherent in the evidence of events and that history is a constructed narrative. This construction of 'truth' is so 'real' that 'foundational' status has been conferred upon it. Foundational history did put a premium on a methodology based on the external nature of objectivity, realism and truth which traditional historians take as their essentials.

It is becoming more and more apparent that difficulties arise in describing the past or the present. Obviously, the world/past comes to us as various stories which we interpret and out of which we can never break. It could be said that history is nothing but historiography, a matrix of reading practices that engage dialectically with existing texts representing an assortment of culturally constructed forms of knowledge, beliefs, codes and customs.[17] Each writing is coloured by the discourse of somebody else.

Is history, then, an art or a science, and is it really possible to declare what happened in the past without a bias? What is the nature of historiography in a postmodernist world? Should history abandon the search for objective truth about the past? Construction, reconstruction and deconstruction are all exercises in the evaluation of the past. These probing questions may be linked to recent currents in theoretical thinking which have given rise to a heated debate on the authenticity of history writing and produced a contested terrain for a conceptual discussion of history. It is time that history came to terms with its own processes of production.

History and Literature

To resolve these questions, one can first look at the lack of concern for a theory of history which is most conspicuous when one moves from the shelves of history to those of literary theory. The short-sightedness of much canonical history comes mainly from the methodology of 'naïve realism' on which it bases itself. The occasional text on theory is often ignored by orthodox historians or not considered seriously in the way literary theory pays attention to works of literature.

It must be acknowledged that although the narrative is borrowed from oral and written testimonies and historical narratives, it is literary and rhetorical. Meanings are an effect of the narrative design, rather than a deduction from facts. It is clear that historical narratives 'have much more in common with fictional narrative than historians are normally willing to allow.'[18] The institutionalised boundaries between history and literature can be challenged by showing that the historical discourse is subject to the same kind of analysis as any other discourse. We may also venture to say that reality is always structured by the text, be it literary or historical, since no writing is transparent.

In this context, one could fall back on Hayden White's view that many teachers of literature often treat the study of the historical context of a literary work as 'a kind of archetype of the realistic pole of representation', alleging that this historical context has a concreteness and an accessibility that the literary work can never have.[19] The presumption of the objectivity and accessibility of the historical milieu makes them forget that the contexts of the very texts that literary scholars study 'are themselves products of the fictive capabilities of the historians who have studied those contexts.'[20]

It is an anathema to theorists like Hayden White that history should vary from the literary or rhetorical aesthetic creation, and they would, therefore, like to expose its literariness so that it has no distinction from philosophy or literature, and is apparently an imaginative creation of the past that goes well beyond the constraints of documents and 'facts'. Any essentialist prig here meets his final collapse.

One reason for the subordination of literature is its institutionalisation in the nineteenth century. The present 'organization of literary studies in the university (by national languages and historical periods) reflects that subservience and association. The collapse of historical philosophies in the aftermath of 1848 provoked a revival of eighteenth-century attempts to divide the sphere of knowledge into clearly demarcated territories subject to different criteria of validity.'[21] From now on literature would be considered in conjunction with aesthetics and as an altogether separate discipline from social history.

But with the recent debates on the 'slipperiness' of language and its 'deep structure', the historian begins to get apprehensive about the epistemological basis of study, and the literary critic deeply wobbly about the idea of history acting as a stable foundation to the world of imagination. As we well know, the signifying power of language disables any attempt to produce a scientific discourse. This is the result of the French deconstructivist school which, together with the Anglo-American analytical school that emphasised the textuality and not the referentiality of a text as the true determinant of historical meaning, produced a popular school of thought. This school proposed that history, in spite of its use of footnotes, quotations and a chronology that stands on the foundations of the canon* of documentation, is, after all, bound by language. This most certainly is a significant development in the philosophy of history because it endeavours to privilege literary discourse by virtue of its self-reflexivity and perceives that the only discernible 'truth' is fiction. The denial of both the fixity of interpretation and the supremacy of any canon is thus asserted in a postmodernist stance. One could argue that there is no reality principle in the writing of history which has a complexion relative to the pleasure or the ideology of the historian. Such an enterprise becomes anti-positivistic and deeply sceptical of absolute truths.

Said and History

Controversies concerning objectivity or subjectivity, singularity or plurality, relativity or universality of truth, abound in the revisionist post-Orientalist historiography which treats areas of knowledge, culture and tradition as sites of conflict. Its main purpose is freedom from essentialism. Apparently, this is a reaction to Western anthropologists and ethnographists who have traditionally followed the conservative assumption that culture is a sphere of privileged social expression. It is this history and the writing of it that has given rise to recent exchanges between the foundationalists and the post-foundationalists, the modernists and the post-modernists. And behind these debates, Said sees the struggle to reformulate variant identities and unstable polities.

Said's writings have contributed substantially to the history/theory debate in the last two decades. By taking truth to be only situational and political, he

opens up the discipline of history to subaltern*
writing and intervention. Said does not fully reject
the validity of the empirical method, but his mar-
shalling of facts, and emphasis on the iconography
of signs, symbols and language, helps to provide the
social and literary historian with a wider vision of
history. Although it is unfair to say that all accounts
of the past are false, Said sets out to demonstrate
that different writings of European scholars were
shaped by ideological and political exigencies of
empire-building, with racial and cultural superiority
inherent in the palpable designs of their political aims.

Representation

The areas of historiography and representation are
vital to Said's writings owing to their problematic
nature in the area of textuality. Our understanding
of the past has been hugely enlarged and deepened
by Said's analysis of literature and culture which
throws light on different classes of people and large
categories of experience that we were unaware of.
Said offers alternative epistemological systems to
dislocate our eurocentric perspective which is shaped
by Western literature and histories. His final purpose is to stress the political character of all such literary pursuit. He has drawn from his long teaching

experience to expose the problematic relationship between literature and history in his two books, *Orientalism* and *Culture and Imperialism*. Said focuses his attention on the intervention of history and literature in historical writing itself, showing how literary narratives and politics are inextricably bound up in the texts of Jane Austen's *Mansfield Park*, Conrad's *Heart of Darkness* and Verdi's opera *Aida*. As he argues in *Culture and Imperialism*:

I suggested that studying the relationship between the 'West' and its dominated cultural 'others' is not just a way of understanding an unequal relationship between unequal interlocutors, but also a point of entry into studying the formation and meaning of Western cultural practices themselves. And the persistent disparity in power between the West and non-West must be taken into account if we are accurately to understand cultural forms like that of the novel, of ethnographic and historical discourse, certain kinds of poetry and opera, where allusions to and structures based on this disparity abound.[22]

On the other hand, post-Orientalist history writing attempts to demystify this delusive enterprise which conceals 'its ideological structure behind a scholarly facade of footnotes and the pretense of facts'.[23] But it is equally vital that all such representations promulgated in the name of 'authentic' and 'true' accounts are also questioned, and their authority and coherence closely re-examined. As Said writes:

Stories are at the heart of what explorers and novelists say about strange regions of the world; they also become the method colonized people use to assert their own identity and the existence of their own history.[24]

This bifocal view that any writing is always a representation brings into play the creative combination of fact and fiction, hinting at the multitudinous and infinite possibilities of writing.

Representing reality from either side can never be an ideologically neutral activity. Said realises the problem of representation in contemporary historical and mythico-religious contexts, fully aware how they falsify and caricature and demean. His work becomes part of a larger body of theoretical analysis which spells out the understanding of ideologies behind the writing of history and the use of materialist criticism in coming to grips with the literary mode of production. Exercising considerable influence on the direction of literary studies in universities around the world, Said has helped to turn 'reading against the grain' into a critical methodology that, at one level, reconciles with postmodernist thinking, and, at another, warns literary theoreticians to take a sceptical view of the lapses into extreme relativism. There is a deep-seated concern in Said with keeping ideological phenomena at the forefront of dialectical analysis. His emphasis is on the adoption of a more globally oriented stance that rejects totalising viewpoints and academic compartmentalising to subvert the intentions of the author.

One may relate the earlier alignment of Said's liberal humanist cultural tradition imbibed from Erich Auerbach and Lionel Trilling with the larger concerns of contemporary literary theory and its post-Enlightenment loss of faith in 'origins', 'centre' and 'end'. Implicit here is the notion of unequal relationships of economic and political power that work behind myths of representations about the Orient, which are integral to the European discourse and its material civilisation. Without this discourse analysis,

one cannot possibly understand the enormously systematic discipline by which European culture was able to manage – and even produce – the Orient politically, sociologically, militarily, ideologically, scientifically, and imaginatively during the post-Enlightenment period.[25]

But first, the influences.

Foucault's Power/Knowledge and Discourse

One of the finest examples of the application of 'high' theory to the discipline of cultural history can be seen in Said's writings. His methodology has enabled him to amalgamate the older Marxist tradition with current critical practice in discourse analysis for the understanding of the relationship between imperialism and culture. This draws him to argue that 'true' accounts of history are only the results of cultural strategies geared to the retention of power and material gain. In projecting his views on culture and histories that are deeply influenced by the dominant ideology and the political essentials of the society in question, Said relies especially on Michel Foucault, Antonio Gramsci and Noam Chomsky. Chomsky's critical interventions have taught him to have the courage to speak on issues that affect us most, more so on the political activity of a community. But whereas Chomsky is interested more in writing directly on political affairs, Said moves towards theorising on what concerns him and his world. In this regard, he is closer to Foucault than to Chomsky, although Chomsky's political commitment overshadows Foucault's cynicism of any direct political involvement.

Orientalism owes a great debt to Foucault's enumerations of the nexus between power and knowledge. Said regards Foucault's 'presentation of the order, stability, authority, and regulatory power of knowledge'[26] as the underpinning notion of all institutions of governance. This is seen to be in operation in disciplinary institutions such as the bureaucracy or the technocracy which are always engaged in strategies of overcoming and co-opting with only one aim – domination.

Foucault's model of power and knowledge is derived from Nietzschean philosophy. It explains very clearly that knowledge is used by agencies wielding power which have at their disposal the established language structures through which all forms of imposition on society are made. What is 'truth' is decided by this powerful minority: it regiments and systematically regulates the subject to suit its own goals by operating through a discourse.

It must be kept in mind that there are mainly two conceptions of power which have dominated discourse studies: power as a simple quantitative capacity to act, and power as resting on consent, and therefore involving also the right to act.[30] Both these conceptions are important for a more comprehensive understanding of discourse formation.

Having talked about power and knowledge, let us examine what Foucault means by discourse. When a linguist talks of the discourse of advertisement, he simply means the formal treatment of the subject in speech or writing, but, in the hands of a philosopher or a social psychologist, the discourse of racism, say, would have entirely different connotations from simply the aspect of verbal communication. Though discourse cannot be pinned down to one meaning, one could step beyond the linguistic connotations of the now very fashionable term. It could be said that at a given moment in the history of a nation, there will always be a particular discourse, a set of rules or conventions that govern the workings of society. The fashioning of a discourse is always controlled and organised by disciplines and institutions which act as agencies for the distribution of codes of conduct and other social procedures. Discourse gives rise to dominant ideas that are responsible for the strict control exercised in society, almost in the nature of the 'panopticon' (a circular prison invigilated by a single warden at the centre) that is responsible for the surveillance of a society according to the dictates of the élites.[31]

As Foucault writes:

Instead of gradually reducing the rather fluctuating meaning of the word 'discourse', I believe I have in fact added to its meanings: treating it sometimes as the general domain of all statements, sometimes as an individualizable group of statements, and sometimes as a regulated practice that accounts for a number of statements.[32]

Foucault first takes discourse as all utterances which have some effect in society and then moves on to look at the particular group of utterances which together have a coherence and power to control. There can thus be a discourse of Orientalism, of femininity, or of race.

Said uses the Foucauldian scheme to bring together a diverse body of texts from politics, literature, linguistics, ethnography and history to create the discourse of Orientalism. Like Foucault, Said does not stop here; he goes on to look at the structures which lie behind the production of texts or utterances that are seemingly more vital to the understanding of the strategies of knowledge, power and control aimed at creating the Orient.

Foucault and, before him, Mikhail Bakhtin give full importance to the centrality of ideology as an embodiment of beliefs, values and categories that constitute a way of looking at the world. Louis Althusser's 'Ideology and Ideological State Apparatuses' (1970) also emphasises that ideologies lie behind consciousness and that they are 'systems of meaning that install everybody in imaginary relations to the real relations in which they live'.[33] The relationship between ideology and discourse gives a significant direction to our understanding of Said. Ideology is more of an overtly political term implying 'a simplistic and negative process whereby individuals were duped into using conceptual systems which were not in their own interests.'[34] On the other hand, discourse, owing to its overt detachment from political affiliations, may be linked to Gramscian hegemony, in which people are complicit in their own subordination.

The Impact of Foucault

Clearly, power is inherently related to the concepts of ideology and discourse, enunciated most ardently by Foucault whose views on the relations between the rulers and the ruled have inspired many literary and social critics to aspire to answer questions on 'who can cause whom to do what'.[35] Rather than only academise the results of his highly interesting research, Said put his ideas to a politically active use in order to raise the political consciousness of at least those who sincerely believed in the idea of democracy.

Said pays full attention to Foucault's notion of discourse that simulates reality perfectly and convincingly by effecting 'domains of objects and rituals of truth'.[36] As we shall see, the East gets transformed into a discursive 'Orient' by the dominant West in all imperial histories. Said has his disagreements with Foucault, however, pertaining to his view that there is no conscious force operating behind power. Foucault's conception of repressive structures refuses to look at the idea of power as a preconceived hegemonic force that always operates hierarchically downwards from an institution of the state located at the top.[37] He emphasises the 'impersonal element' in the operation of power that has for its goal the fashioning of subjects and their histories. For Said, this is not so; he maintains instead that there is a conscious plan and intentionality behind the Western domination of the East. Governments, authors, individuals are not simply the passive agents of such strategies.

Further, while Foucault is keenly interested in offering a theory of domination, the 'contestatory' or 'oppositional' aspect of social forces is absent from his thinking. Struggles are conducted for evolving and producing a system of discourse, but Foucault cares little for the success of counter-discursive practices. Insofar as resistance strategies are concerned, Said upholds the relevance of Antonio Gramsci and Raymond Williams. He argues that it is wrong to call these counter-discursive practices 'non-systemic' because the writings of Fanon, Syed Alatas, Abdallah Laroui, Panikkar, Shariati, and novelists like Ngugi wa Thiong'o and Salman Rushdie, as well as all writings appearing from the minority cultures, have an inherent subversive force to protest and speak up for the subaltern. No power, therefore, is invincible and unidirectional. Said quotes Williams to corroborate his disagreement with Foucault and assent with Gramsci that

however dominant a social system may be, the very meaning of its domination involves a limitation or selection of the activities it covers, so that by defini-

tion it cannot exhaust all social experience, which therefore always potentially contains space for alternative acts and alternative intentions which are not yet articulated as a social institution or even power.[38]

For the theoretical basis of his argument, Said uses Foucault's *History of Sexuality* and *Discipline and Punish*. But he is equally dependent upon Gramsci for his creative use of 'hegemony', although he modifies the term to suit his projected thesis.

Said and Gramsci

Gramsci's idea of hegemony links the spontaneous consent of the masses to the maintenance of power by a minority class through the use of persuasion and collaboration. This consent is caused by the aura and prestige of the dominant fundamental group which constantly manipulates its social and political strategies to maintain the acceptance of class society which otherwise should turn revolutionary in response to such hegemony. Hegemony implies both control through consent as well as the awareness of spasmodic cases of subversion which are always present in the hegemonised society.

Gramscian hegemony, through the subtle and

even unconscious use of persuasion, sways the populace. To achieve this, the imposition of language, and, through it, the writing of literature and history, play a significant role in setting up systems and institutions that perpetuate and consolidate the ideology of the dominant class. British literature and history, for instance, as well as the English language – the carrier of Englishness – have the function of disseminating ideas that help in contributing to the hegemonic domination of one class by another.

The ideas of Gramsci as they evolved in the context of his position as one of the major leaders of the Italian working-class movement, and the way in which they took shape during his long imprisonment under fascism, led to a reappraisal of cultural, artistic and literary forces. Said depends upon Gramsci's major work, *Selections From Prison Notebooks*, for his project on the rise of Orientalism. The defence of democratic culture is central to the understanding of this project of responding to imperial/fascist histories.

Hegemony works best by creating the confusion of contradictory ideas in the minds of the masses as they absorb cultural values and beliefs of the dominating class. It tends to make the subaltern 'accept inequality and oppression as natural and unchangeable'.[39] It is this Gramscian notion of 'common sense' that enables the West to create myths of power and dominance. 'Common sense' is purely a negative term in the Gramscian lexicon as it becomes the site of ideological construction. Gramsci calls for a criticism of this inculcation of 'common sense' which, for Said, is the task of a 'contrapuntal' critic who reveals the nature of ideological resistance. Said's borrowings from Gramsci enable him to give an added dimension to the study of both imperialist historical accounts and cultural resistance, and to finally understand the theory of political power as well as the revolutionary processes in the making of history. Such a view of history offers a critique of cultural change in terms of colonialism and of the notion of a single linear narrative in any trajectory of history.

In these myths of power, the subaltern critic has to decipher the combination of coercion and persuasion behind the organisation of political and ideological leadership. It must be understood that Gramsci draws a contrast between *egemonia* (hegemony) and *dominazione* (domination). He turns the notion of hegemony-as-strategy to hegemony-as-concept, a tool for understanding society in order to change it. Hegemony has a 'national-popular dimension as well as a class dimension' and requires 'the unification of a variety of different social forces into a broad alliance expressing a national-popular collective will'.[40]

Viewed from this standpoint, colonial discourse is itself a process of extensive reorganisation which is needed to establish Western hegemony. It is a way of transmuting popular ways of thinking and feeling, of people's conceptions of themselves, their moral standards and their history. A wholesale transformation of popular consciousness brought about by Western hegemony serves the purpose of stabilising foreign rule.

Said's theoretical concerns deal with positions of ideology and Marxist aesthetics within a literary context. He sees the literary texts and the historical accounts of the West as valuable representations of the ways in which hegemony works. He uses his 'deconstructive' analysis of different European texts as a template to spur a subaltern interpretation which would make possible an understanding of the methods used for oppression and their reproduction in literature or music. Ideas thus become the place of power relations and knowledge which work in tandem with the maintenance of power. Said uses Gramsci to emphasise the need for intellectuals to react strongly against any authoritarian practice and be aware of the strategies of the repressive myths of hegemony.

Said's writings under the influence of Gramsci have a continuing relevance at a time of widespread withdrawal from Marxist positions among those on the postmodern Left. Gramsci's theory of cultural production and critique when applied to Said bring out the relevant issues of social domination and the subversion that takes place continuously to resist any fixed notions of cultural behaviour.

Said's cultural criticism has, in fact, rescued Marxist thinking from the determinism and economic reductionism to which it had fallen prey. He has taken the Gramscian model for the writing of revisionist history where his foremost concern is the notion of the materiality of ideas, the theorising on political praxis, and the concept of hegemony which had mainly one common underlying suggestion: the vitality of language as a dramatic and active social construction that plays a material role in creating the social history of the world. For Gramsci, as for Said, history is not 'preordained' since it can be influenced by ideas and not by economics alone, as maintained by orthodox Marxists. Neither Gramsci nor Said gives any importance to universal ideas, since they believe that all events and ideas are historicised and contextualised in time and place.

Said versus the Enlightenment Project

While specifically highlighting problems of discourse analysis within the field of colonial history, Said has more recently challenged definitions of literature and the construction of Western knowledge which are centrally located in the hegemonic liberal-humanist project called the Enlightenment. The Enlightenment project emphasised Reason and Progress which could only issue forth from the Western mind. Said shows that the Enlightenment ideals of Reason and Progress had a hidden agenda: that of creating a successful imperial practice. If the rest of the world was made to believe in a superior (and enduring) set of human laws, imperialism would flourish unreservedly.

In the broad science of colonialism, culture was made to operate with the motive of obtaining consent from the colonised. Matthew Arnold's famous 1860s adage of 'the best that has been known and thought' was both an Enlightenment premise and a liberal-humanist sanction which were used to justify colonialism. It was made to look as if the victim was in need of such an influence and not the perpetrator. According to the ruler's argument, it was the barbarism of the African or the Indian which required their inevitable occupation. It was necessary, they argued, for Europeans to fulfil the 'civilising mission' since the barbarians beseeched colonialism.

This set of overarching beliefs rested on the 'knowledge' about the fixed, constant and essentialist character of human nature. The result was the production of an unshakeable 'discourse' that the inferior races would continue to remain as unprogressive as they had been.

European culture thus spread its unquestioned acceptability through having its superiority universally recognised. Such a political ideology gives imperceptible approval to cultural production, leaving it always uncontested. It is for this reason that the violence of imperialism was never interrogated by the traditional intellectuals, who, in certain cases, lent support to the enterprise through their writings.

Recent anti-foundationalist histories show that the Enlightenment project was contingent upon the circumstantial and provisional aspect of social construction. We are now toying with the opposite idea that there can never be any disinterested inquiry or objective sets of assumptions.

Said and Orientalism

Recent explosions in scholarly research on the subject of imperialism have shown the consequences of the European colonial enterprise, of the ways in which the West looks for power structures they can understand and advance; if they do not discover one, they construct one.

An Orient was created as an object of study through the discoveries of ancient texts, literature, philology and anthropology which intentionally emphasised difference and distinctiveness, and ended up dehumanising the societies under study. Orientalism was never a disinterested science, but operated on the premise of unequal relations with the motive of determining how lands could be occupied and managed. The underlying dogmas were persistent in their assumption that the Orient was aberrant, underdeveloped, inferior and incapable of defining itself.[41] Such scholarship, based on the philosophical category of the centre, which finally develops into the larger concept of eurocentrism, is, according to Said, morally bankrupt and fundamentally destructive.[42]

In *Orientalism*, Said uses two epitaphs. The first one, from Disraeli's 1847 novel *Tancred*, says: 'The East is a career.' The other is from Marx's description of the ordinary farmer in *The Eighteenth Brumaire of Louis Bonaparte*: 'They cannot represent themselves; they must be represented.' Said is here ironically subverting the very project of metropolitan hegemony in the invention of imperial history. In other words, he offers a critique of the whole practice of representation which can never be final or 'true'.

Said gives a three-fold definition of Orientalism. The first, and the simplest, defines Orientalism as an academic study of the Orient by Western scholars. Making use of Foucault's celebrated concept of power/knowledge, Said links this definition to a second: that this study creates a body of knowledge which the more pragmatic and utilitarian among Western imperialists use as a means of gaining power. To take an example, Said would argue that the academic interest in Oriental languages inspired by the Sanskrit scholar, Sir William Jones, was hijacked by utilitarian Englishmen for political ends. The entire field of study along with its scholarly institutions was anything but disinterested. That the study of the Orient became an active, self-generating discipline in the nineteenth century, which marks the peak of colonial expansion, lends credence to Said's argument that knowledge about the East is the beginning of a discourse about power.

Said also explores a third interpretation: the making of epistemological and ontological distinctions between the East and the West which perpetuate the stereotypes of developed/barbaric, advanced/primitive, superior/inferior, rational/aberrant, and so on, all of which fall into the larger binaries of 'self' and 'other'. Developing Foucault's ideas in *Discipline and Punish*, *Madness and Civilization* and *The Order of Things*, Said explains how the 'other' has to be constructed, and even fabricated, to generate a belief in the 'self'. The East thus becomes a surrogate 'self' that Western scholars do not choose to acknowledge; essentialisms such as cruelty, sensuality, decadence, etc. are always taken to be characteristics of the 'exotic other'. It also tends to be seen as homogeneous – the people there being anonymous masses rather than individuals.

The subtle use of stereotypes, hinging obsessively on the violent and sensual nature of the natives, made legitimate a very cruel and exploitative practice of colonialism. The coloniser could justify subjugation and even extermination through the logic of the 'civilising mission' which in Rudyard Kipling's rhetoric became the 'white man's burden'.

Orientalism is inherently made up of a number of discourses that continuously jostle with each other, producing an absorptive science whose main motive is to use knowledge and power to produce its object of study. Examples abound in the Victorian travelogue which conceives of the East as 'a grand harem' with endless possibilities for pleasure and perversion, ripe for colonisation. The travel narrative, with its exaggerated information and fantastic accounts of far away lands, produced an ethnological discourse of immense significance as it offered information about the native cultures that were to be subdued. Rider Haggard's *King Solomon's Mines* is another account of Western imperialism and its accompanying patriarchal discourse that sets out to take control over the colonised woman, a material commodity at the disposal of the dominant power. Gender here becomes something more than just a sexual category; it takes on the semantics of not only labour, but exploitation and control.[43]

Within the Western discourse, Muslim princesses were represented as perfidious, debauched and self-seeking so as to show the hollowness of a living different from an upright Christian sense of morality. It was argued that whereas the Christian world stood for disembodied heaven, the East envisaged a heaven of lust and greed. The travellers often described the East as hedonistic, a place where the white man could get a ready supply of lusty slaves and harems full of passionate women. The sexual history of British imperial rule shows how the attitudes to sex of young men fresh from school were of exotic sexual adventure, of possessing mistresses and enjoying visits to brothels.[44]

In Shakespeare, the East would stand for the gratification of the senses, sexual desire and oblivion from the affairs of the world, the sum of which is embodied in the image of Cleopatra. Rome, in contrast, stands for the edifice of trust, respectability and Empire. Antony, torn between the West and the East, enters into a political marriage with the 'wise' Octavia but cannot give up Cleopatra who 'makes hungry where she most satisfies'. Cleopatra in her barge represents 'the Orient created for the western gaze', a prototype of the seductive Eastern woman, royal and desirable, a temptress who lures the Western explorer.[45]

Undoubtedly, a representation of the indolent and sensual native would permit the imperialists to justify to the sedentary reader back home that their honourable mission was to civilise the barbaric East and thereby acquire popular sanction to subjugate entire continents. The 'cosmetic cant of *mission civilisatrice*' served to forge the imperial representation of the world. History, reason and science were deployed to meet the ends of its governance without making the obvious mistake of sounding either exploitative or unduly xenophobic.[46]

Other obvious examples are Tarzan, the aristocratic Anglo-Saxon Baden-Powell's vision of the Boy Scouts, Iago's reference to Othello as a 'Barbary horse', all of which perpetuate the crude stereotype of the primitive man with a blatant emphasis on the superiority of the white race over the apathetic, cowardly and treacherous Oriental.[47]

These types of racist thinking were akin to the Victorian views on class difference and fed the personal idiosyncrasies of the Europeans, enabling them to sustain the political structure at home. Orientalist studies would give power and knowledge to the conqueror to uphold the Empire. The Western narrative paradigm in which the author-anthropologist fashions the 'other' is a form of domination created through a hegemonic discourse formation whose sensationalism and inaccuracy is now being questioned through the revisionist programmes of historians and postcolonial cultural critics. As Albert Memmi would argue, colonisation implies a removal from one's history.[48] It follows that European-made history as an imperial construct has to be questioned in order to undo Western hegemony and 'its ideological acceptance of error as truth'.[49]

The deconstruction of Europe's myths of the Orient within the context of recent political and geographical upheavals throws up new configurations and transfigurations of Orientalism, each internally complex, contradictory and unstable. The condition of discursive formations, as Foucault argues, is always dynamic and discontinuous, not unchanging, static or uniform. Said uses this argument to explain the semantics of the Orient and the Occident which inevitably always includes a variety of heterogeneous positions.

In explaining Said's stand, it has to be seen how divergent interpretations are necessary to perceive the heterogeneity of the Arabs or the Indians, as the case may be. The emergence of pluralism, both in the realm of political and aesthetic value, and in the sphere of human knowledge, has called into question philosophical monism, the doctrine that all reality and knowledge forms a rational, harmonious whole and that there is ultimate unity between human ends.

This has brought attention to the need to construct a new canon of history writing by not only rewriting history, but also re-interpreting the psychodynamics of Western texts in such a way that areas of subterranean cultural politics may be brought to the surface. Conventions of literary realism are to be questioned; close readings of the opera and the novel made to bring out hidden sub-texts of historical data and biased non-literary material that no authority can possibly conceal or subjugate. Such sniping at the centres of power through a methodology that is transgressive reacts against the overarching generalisations of history. It increases the available range of interpretations by constantly exposing the fascist ideology behind the humanist categories of 'normalcy', 'order' and 'origins', thereby giving the area of postcolonial cultural practice and colonial discourse analysis a theoretical respectability.

Some critics of the fundamentalist Islamic or Hindu variety have, however, taken refuge in the notion of a homogeneous and pristine identity ostensibly sanctioned by *Orientalism*. By partly endorsing Said's Orientalist model, they work on the assumption that 'native' histories are 'authentic' and 'real'.[50] Any criticism of their belief results in fatwas because such interpretations pose a threat to their sacred texts or perpetuate doubts about the 'true' version of religion.

It comes as no surprise that the Derridian disbelief in logocentrism or 'master narratives' endangers the community of both faithful Muslims and staunch Orientalists. Said vehemently disagrees with both positions by objecting that such 'approaches represent a heterogeneous dynamic and complex human reality from an uncritically essentialist standpoint'.[51] Said supports neither the idea of an 'enduring oriental reality' nor that of an immutable Western essence. History is by its very nature dynamic and fluid and this has to be considered in countering Orientalism, in which scholarship is aligned with military power for the final purpose of establishing the empire.

What's Wrong with *Orientalism*?

There are some methodological problems within Said's hypothesis of Orientalism. It is felt that the study of a systematic and unitary attitude to the East is too monolithic and dismisses with a single sweep the inconsistencies and varieties of Western orientalisms as practised by the English, the French, the Spanish and the Portuguese. Moreover, the totalising force of Western discourse is rejected as 'inauthentic', with the implicit assumption that there is a representation which is real. Yet, attempts at representing indigenous cultures invariably turn out to be orientalisms in reverse. As Dennis Porter puts it: 'Orientalism in one form or another is not only what we have but all we can ever have.'[52] Critics also claim that the argument in *Orientalism* is contradictory, since the very force which Said critiques is later upheld in the subaltern critics.

It may also be alleged that Said is critical of the canon but upholds his faith in Western great works. The important issue to keep in mind is the role of the individual who not only aligns himself 'with the emergent working class against ruling hegemony' but is also 'eminently useful in making hegemony work'.[53] A culture that produces such 'organic intellectuals' and preserves Matthew Arnold's legacy would necessarily uphold certain canonical works.[54] And surprisingly, Said gives evidence of being in favour of the Western canon consisting of Swift, Austen, Dickens, Yeats and Conrad, among others. He suspects these very institutions of culture for producing a literary Orient yet at the same time advocates them. It is on this treacherous ground that Aijaz Ahmad attacks him. On the one hand,

Said notes the complicity of High Humanism with the colonial project. On the other, Said's urgings towards 'sympathy, constituency, affiliation and filiation' align him closely with humanism's notions of cultural relativism and accommodation. Ahmad says: 'What is remarkable about this at times very resounding affirmation of humanist values is that humanism-as-ideality is involved precisely at the time when humanism-as-history has been rejected so unequivocally.'[55]

The combination of Western humanism and Nietzschean rejection of established truths is theoretically a disastrous strategy for a cosmopolitan critic engaged in debates of both a political and literary nature and those concerning the Middle East. But it goes to Said's credit that although he finds distortions in the construction of the East, he also accepts that reconstructions from the East are questionable. Does he not take up these very texts to expose and oppose their imperialist forms and strategies?[56]

Said takes the prevailing categories of history to be so deeply complicit with the imperialist system of meaning and values that they become obstacles in the path of representations written in opposition to such hegemonic practice. Through the modified

about the empire were always fortified by the English novel which, according to him, is an important organ of cultural formation, a repertoire of liberal humanist values needed to civilise the 'other'. The British novel and the expanding empire worked in tandem, aiding each other. A product of the nineteenth-century bourgeois society, the novel always gave unquestionable endorsement to British overseas policy.

Take, for instance, Jane Austen's *Mansfield Park*. Said's reading of it goes beyond the canonical view which either speaks of Austen's lack of interest in colonial history or of her exaggerated concerns with domestic issues. Said contextualises the novel within the areas of private domination and slavery. Sir Thomas Bertram's absence from Mansfield Park for taking care of his agricultural enterprise in Antigua is necessary to maintain a certain order and a lifestyle back home; trade in slaves and sugar takes care of prosperity on the domestic front where the ambience of the imperialist culture pervades every aspect of life. This referring back to the content of the novel from a colonial perspective, in order to decipher almost invisible sub-texts that constantly prop up attitudes towards imperialism, is the 'contrapuntal' method that Said uses to deconstruct the often disregarded ideas lying buried in fiction.

Said's purpose is not to brand Jane Austen as a British agent of imperialism or lay bare her role in showing the violence of British colonial rule. He wants to highlight the generic nature of the novel which takes imperialism as natural and inevitable within the context of British culture. He is concerned with exposing the leisured class that relished Austen's fiction and absent-mindedly accepted the perpetuation and fruits of the empire.

Similarly, Said regards Verdi's opera *Aida* as a work of art which advances imperialism and consolidates domination through generating a favourable public opinion both in the metropolitan centres and the marginalised Third World communities. Like *Mansfield Park*, the network of affiliations with the imperial doctrine becomes apparent through a contrapuntal reading of the opera, in which Said finds a link between its subject matter and the conflict in the foreign policy of Italy, France and Britain. Egypt was backed by Britain to undertake a military invasion into Ethiopia, where the Italians and the French also had colonial ambitions. Written by an Italian, the opera carries the implicit view that Egypt is the aggressor and the villain. The British foreign policy is thereby critiqued. The opera, as Said argues, is 'an imperial spectacle designed to alienate and impress an almost exclusively European audience'.[57] We see here a vivid example of how culture and politics unite to bestow a sense of centrality to European arts and ideas. What is remarkable is how these cultural forms gain social sanction and appropriation without revealing the reality of their imperial motivations. This is a good example of how hegemony operates.

Rudyard Kipling's *Kim* is another case in point which should be treated as a text that serves not merely as an account of the Indian way of life, but as an imperialist rationale of domination over a 'delinquent' land. Britain in the novel stands for justice and control which is so indispensable for an 'unruly' and 'wild' country like India. A fictionalised India is thus fabricated to uphold British supremacy as an inevitable need for its 'modernisation'.

This is Said's method of showing that domination of the world is socially and academically made acceptable when assisted by popular culture, fiction, painting and opera. Each of these becomes an interweaving of various discourses, each being read through a deconstructive strategy against itself, with the reliability of meaning harassed and subverted continuously.

Being an enthusiastic lover of classical music and

aware of its theory, Said's criticism becomes the study of dissonance and tension between aesthetic, cultural and historical approaches. The textual traces from the past, although minute, are never overlooked so that the intention, genre and historical situation are given equal importance. The production and consumption of written material involves social and ideological struggles containing shifts in value and interest. This is vital to Said's methodology.

Culture and Imperialism is significant for its global range and scholarly references that give the reader a well-researched and imaginatively recreated history of the last two centuries of European imperialism, stretching from Romanticism to the contemporary postcolonial/postmodern scenario, with the intervening period of nationalist struggles of modernism. This cosmopolitan overview of history does not ignore the continuing prevalence of fundamentalist/nativist tendencies in the Third World. Third World oppositional narratives are always present struggling to be heard. Consent and resistance lie at the heart of Said's thesis on culture and its relationship to imperialism. The contradictions which one can detect here stem from his ambiguous relationship with postmodernism. He rejects totalising narratives and yet often castigates contemporary theory extending from discourse analysis to deconstruction. Contradictions of the secular and the religious, the linear and the contrapuntal, drive home his critical methodology which underscores his dislocation and multiple positioning. Any attempt at resolving these polarities would in all probability be falling back into the arms of absolutist or linear master narratives. But the emphasis on the simultaneity of conjunctions and disjunctions is the basis of his historical approach. The streak of postmodernism in him, therefore, cannot be denied.

Mapping Resistance and Subalternity

Said's contrapuntal methodology does not limit itself to the analysis of only Western writings. The ideology of resistance is basic to it. Using an alien language, the colonised writer reconstructs and reframes the cultural reality expressed in Western discourse. More than a mere oppositionality, there is a recreation and recontextualising of history written from a linear and univocal perspective. Such a project aims at the recovery of one's identity and history that has been 'infiltrated by the culture of empire'.[58]

In order to counter the bias perpetuated by eurocentric norms, and its view of the pre-colonial era as a pre-civilisational limbo, a need for 'cultural resistance', such as Fanon had earlier endorsed in *The Wretched of the Earth*, becomes imperative. Characteristically, therefore, the postcolonial critic who traces his ancestry to Fanon and Said evokes a native version of his pre-colonial history.

Said feels that in *Orientalism* he overlooked the response of resistance which was to climax 'in the great movement of decolonization all across the Third World'.[59] This gives rise to important voices which ceaselessly shape and remould surviving parameters of power and knowledge. The writings of Chinua Achebe and Ngugi wa Thiong'o, Africa's foremost novelists, for example, are replete with assertions of counter-discursive practice which become sites for opposing paradigms. Achebe's *Things Fall Apart* and *Arrow of God* reflect the organisation of Igbo society in Nigeria and the roles and power structures inherent in it. The literary text is seen as more than just an exercise in reflecting poetics and rhetoric; its very aesthetics are born out of a *political* concern to assert black aesthetics, as well as to counterpose indigenous institutions, cosmography and oral traditions against the unfair hegemonic impact of an alien culture. The tension in these novels offsets any totalising tendencies of Western traditional literary criticism by probing into conflicts, engagements and estrangements between two cultures. In the same way, we see the evidence of subversion in late nineteenth-century Bengali novelists and poets who had ideological and epistemological disagreements with the colonial state.

Even as subversive strategies are prevalent, innumerable nationalist historians continue to write from a wholly Western perspective, implicating themselves in the structures of the former colonialists. Fanon has rightly argued that bourgeois nationalism is transformed into forms of racism and separatism in which the former colonial hegemony is replaced by a dominant ethnic group which perpetuates its power through the legacy of colonial structures. A fundamental mutation comes only through the subaltern movements geared to disregard the interests of the bourgeoisie.

But often, subaltern identities get their impetus from exaggerating the opposition between the Orient and the Occident. The argument in *Orientalism* has been used for xenophobic and race-oriented nationalism in both the Arab and the Hindu world of fundamentalism. Said finds this absolutely undesirable and would prefer that 'the less it was given credit for actually describing any-thing more than a fascinating history of interpreta-tions and of contesting interests, the better.'[60] He, in fact, has only intended to highlight the multicultural practice that runs through the field of historical interpretation. This revisionary and decolonising process of reconstruction, in Saidian terms, does not advocate any chauvinistic or nativist project but is a liberation towards a more persuasive trans-national understanding of one's history through a reappropriation of heterogeneity and hybridity.

Said is concerned to show that opposing strate-gies of power which underpin a contrapuntal read-ing aim at pulling culture and literature out of their narrow concerns into a space of historical inter-mixture. Notions of migrancy, racial and geograph-ical tensions, the unavoidability of the local, and the irreducibility of heterogeneity, counter any essentialisms or universalisms that predominate in Western discourse. As Gyan Prakash writes:

These writings reinterpret identity as a process of ambivalent identification, reopen theories of enclosed histories with accounts of entangled, hierarchical engagements and resituate historical antagonisms in the agonistic process of narrating and rememorizing.[61]

The phenomenon of Orientalism must not be taken as 'a synecdoche, or a miniature symbol, of the entire West'.[62] Nor must the reader of Said take his thesis as any kind of political support for Islamic or Muslim fundamentalism, of which he has been often accused. These right-wing critics take umbrage in such a view that wrongly gives the message that *Orientalism* is based on the binary opposition of two rival camps. Said's claim, it should be understood, balances the development of every culture against 'the existence of another, different and competing *alter ego*'. He writes:

The construction of identity . . . involves the construction of opposites and 'others' whose actuality is always subject to the continuous interpretation and re-interpretation of their differences from 'us'.[63]

Taking a strong Marxist position, he posits the idea of an ever-changing identity that is never impervious to historical, social, intellectual and political processes and contests. History writing, as we have seen, is constrained by the disposition of power and powerlessness and always underpinned with processes of conditioning and socialisation. It is vital that all such representations promulgated in the name of 'authentic' and 'true' accounts are questioned, and their authority and coherence closely re-examined.

Dangers of Anti-foundationalism

But there is one danger lurking here. Every kind of history would marginalise the other race or gender or class. As pointed out by Gertrude Himmelfarb:

To pluralize and particularize history to the point where people share no history in common – no 'generic' history, as it were – is to deny the common (generic) humanity of all people, whatever their sex, race, class, religion and the like. It is also to trivialize history by so fragmenting it that it lacks all coherence and focus, all sense of continuity, indeed all meaning.[64]

And then, if all truth is relative, would not the truth of the racist discourse or the counter-discourse to the reality of Auschwitz be equally legitimate? Is not inequality among races reduced only to 'difference' and pluralism? If postmodernist theory gloats in difference, hybridity and indeterminacy, all of which are important to contemporary writings, how can it answer these questions?

There is, of course, the pervasive problem of nihilism. With the presence of infinite possibilities of meaning, reality almost certainly begins to crumble. However, to say that postmodernist views of history are nihilistic is to miss the main argument: no one has ever denied that history can be written. Postmodernists do not ignore logical arguments, verification and archival research. But neither do they maintain that all interpretations are valid. Postmodernism only asserts that there is never only one meaning. Reason is not forsaken, as is argued by many conventional historians; only its dogmatic representation of itself as timeless certainty is cast aside. Postmodernists question the efficacy of truth since they believe that actuality is only a historical and cultural fabrication. They are not of the view that history is only creative fiction, as is commonly assumed, or that every perspective on the past is as valid as the other. Historians are apparently being urged to be more imaginative and reflexive about their discipline and recognise their creative role in the construction of historical narratives. Thus, hyper-relativism is an ill-founded charge against postmodernist writings.

There is one other problem. Although the connection between the erosion of the universalist claims of

Western epistemology and the increasing impact of other cultures on European thinking is sustained by labels such as 'postmodern', 'postcolonial' and 'poststructural', it may be alleged that these very labels are administered hegemonically to cultures and texts to prevent the infiltration of non-European presence into an ascendant European system. And even though such 'neo-universalisms' constitute liberating practices from the discourse of the coloniser or the master narrative, they have also been interpreted as a shrewd means of controlling the 'other'. The seizure of native literature by such a control that spurs the controversy of 'self' and 'other' brings about the crisis of defining one's own generic forms.

This paradox is significant and cannot be ignored if the indigenous discourse is to discard the imperial by having an authoritativeness of its own. Postcolonial politics has, therefore, to be seen as integral to postmodernism; the practice of history-writing has to be integrated within poststructuralist theorising about representation, subject, gender and the interaction of discourse and power.

Said and the Secular Critic

Said's writings on politics, Western classical music, as well as history and literature, abundantly demonstrate that he is, like Raymond Williams, a cultural critic. As he maintains in his book, *The World, the Text, and the Critic*, if he was to 'use one word consistently along with criticism, it would be oppositional.'[65] He proceeds to elaborate this view:

In its suspicion of totalizing concepts, in its discontent with reified objects, in its impatience with guilds, special interests, imperialized fiefdoms, and orthodox habits of mind, criticism is most itself and, if the paradox can be tolerated, most unlike itself at the moment it starts turning into organized dogma.[66]

Said would like criticism to be 'opposed to every form of tyranny, domination, and abuse' in order to produce a 'non-coercive knowledge' for the good of humanity and its inherent sense of freedom.[67]

In *The World, the Text, and the Critic*, Said underlines the main responsibilities of a critic, foremost among them being the opposition to the hegemonic power of cultural formations. The significance of cultural criticism lies in its refusal to be 'neutered' and its goal to be an instrument of intervention in the unveiling of all struggles for political hegemony. For Said, texts exist in 'circumstances, time, place' and thus 'are in the world, and hence worldly'.[68] Worldliness lies in the connection between the text and the political reality in which it is produced. Said's writing affirms the link between criticism and life as a Palestinian exile (dis)located in the United States, always conscious of his partisan political stance which forms the backdrop to all that he has ideologically believed in. He has fashioned a career out of the texture of his own diasporic dislocation that refuses to get fixed in an essentialised past. Memory, fantasy, narrative and myth continuously interact with history, culture and power, thereby bringing about experiences of continuity and difference.

In a post-narrative mode of history-telling, Said sets out to intervene in the formation of cultures and disallow subjects to become subservient to systems. He had examined the idea of narrativisation first in his doctoral thesis on Conrad at Harvard. Later, he used the thesis in *Beginnings*, and then, with a political slant, in his work on Orientalist strategies. After the completion of his seminal work *Orientalism*, Said began to rewrite the history of the Middle East conflict in *The Question of Palestine* and *Covering Islam*. The subject of these texts conspicuously indicates Said's ideological stand that enables him to correlate history not just with culture and politics but also the 'self'.

Central to Said's argument is the role of the interventionist critic. The author or the critic must be conscious of the role of cultural production in the act of writing. His responsibility lies in exposing the falsity of representations which always conceal a subterranean agenda. This can be achieved through the re-writing of history from a Left-poststructuralist perspective. In *Orientalism*, he re-narrates the story of imperialism that is underpinned by the production of knowledge and through the cultural takeover of the Orient. Here lies the commitment of a conscientious cultural critic and a historian who always intervenes to show how discursive formations arise.

When he applies his theoretical position to practice, he does not neglect the realities of power and authority as well as the ingredients of resistance and subversion which are always present at the heart of any social movement. Like Auerbach, whose *Mimesis* he holds in high esteem, Said feels he is performing 'an act of cultural, even civilizational, survival of the highest importance.'[69] For this reason he has, throughout his academic career, remained anti-essentialist and radically sceptical about categories like Islam or the Orient. Such essentialisms have no stable reality, as all human history is an ideological construction based on 'an odd combination of the empirical and the imaginative'.[70] He further develops this standpoint:

Since the struggle for control over territory is part of that history, so too is the struggle over historical and social meaning. The task for the critical scholar is not to separate one struggle from another, but to connect them, despite the contrast between the overpowering materiality of the former and the apparent otherworldly refinements of the latter.[71]

A literary critic is one who situates himself polemically within the social context and yet tries to move beyond it to interrogate fixed origins. Clearly, Said is not rigid like the poststructuralists who discard all origins. In *Beginnings*, Said argues strongly that all literary texts have inherent 'beginnings'.[72] The author, for Said, is never 'dead'; he is always present with some concrete intention, although social pressures do have a hold on him. For him, the author does not only have a narrow discursive function but possesses all the ingredients of a committed and an active ideological stand. Why else would Said speak of the 'truth' of the Middle East problem and the Palestinian question that he has written so much about? Yet he often rejects narrow fundamentalist and ethnic labels, believing all beginnings to have false origins even as they cannot be wholly rejected. While he cannot deny that he is not a disinterested critic, he also argues that he is secular in all his writings.

So for him, theorising is 'insurrectionary', a practice that rebels against the hegemony of determinism and positivism that have been the traditional strongholds of liberal humanism. But theory also abandons any responsibility for the final formation of cultures or the text. Said takes a dim view of theory's retreat into textuality, for then it begins to oppose and displace the space of history. The obsession with 'textuality' in contemporary literary theory is antithetical to 'secular criticism' that rejects all orthodoxy. The text is a cultural production related to the power systems external and internal to it. Through its power of representation, it speaks of the world around it. If texts are relevant to the understanding of 'real history', how can they be divorced from the world of time and space and the historical moment in which they are located? The 'worldliness' is, therefore, in the text as much as the text is in the world outside it. Said applies this methodology to the analyses of the Orientalist discourse as well as to his views on the Palestinian issue. Contextualising and recontextualising of all texts is vital to the understanding of problems of dispossession, injustice and hypocrisy, particularly for those who have little concern for the arcane vocabulary of theory or the philosophy of ideas.

Said thus directs the critical consciousness towards the secular which would help in inculcating an 'acute sense of what political, social, and human values are entailed in the reading, production, and transmission of every text.'[73] Said, in other words, advocates the notion of resistance to theory:

I would go so far as saying that it is the critic's job to provide resistances to theory, to open it up toward historical reality, toward society, toward human needs and interests, to point up those concrete instances drawn from everyday reality that lie outside or just beyond the interpretive area necessarily designated in advance and thereafter circumscribed by every theory.[74]

In sum, unlike the postmodernist critic, Said believes in the origins of the text which determine the materiality of production as well as the ideological circumstances which have a direct bearing on its form and content. The critic must locate himself in the world outside him without losing sight of the public or social spheres. Such a critic is 'secular' because he moves beyond the narrow confines of his academic professionalism in which it seems there is 'no contact with the world of events and societies, which modern history, intellectuals, and critics have in fact built.'[75] Said advocates the notion of an 'amateur' critic who steps beyond the rules of practical criticism and apolitical literary appreciation to a position where he is not constrained by established literary paradigms. For him, the text, the critic and the public readership are locked in a dialectical relationship.

Notes

1. Edward W. Said, 'Reflections of an Exile', interview with Nikhil Padgaonkar, *Biblio*, vol. 4, Nov–Dec 1999, p. 13.

2. Edward W. Said, 'Representations of the Intellectual' (Reith Lectures), *The Independent*, 24 June 1993, p. 24.

3. Edward W. Said, *Out of Place*, London: Granta, 2000, p. xiv.

4. Ibid., p. 3.

5. Edward W. Said, 'Intellectual Exile: Expatriates and Marginals' (Reith Lectures), *The Independent*, 8 July 1993, p. 16.

6. Salman Rushdie, *Imaginary Homelands: Essays and Criticism 1981–1991*, London: Granta, 1991, p. 376.

7. Cited in Jennifer Wallace, 'Exiled by Foes, Silenced by Friends', *Times Higher Education Supplement*, 17 January 1997, p. 17.

8. Edward W. Said, 'Orientalism Reconsidered', in Francis Barker et al., eds, *Europe and Its Others*, vol. 1, Colchester: University of Essex, 1985, p. 15.

9. Rushdie, *Imaginary Homelands*, p. 13.

10. Edward W. Said, 'Against the Orthodoxies', in Anouar Abdallah, ed., *For Rushdie: Essays by Arab and Muslim Writers in Defense of Free Speech*, New York: George Braziller, 1994, p. 261.

11. See Ernest Gellner, 'The Mightier Pen?', *Times Literary Supplement*, 19 February 1993, p. 3. Gellner vehemently attacks Said for his 'double standards' and 'contradictions'.

12. Cited in Bill Ashcroft and Pal Ahluwalia, *Edward Said: The Paradox of Identity*, London: Routledge, 1999, p. 28.

13. Said, 'Reflections of an Exile', p. 13.

14. Ibid.

15. Ibid.

16. Said, 'Representations of the Intellectual', p. 24.

17. See Keith Jenkins, *Re-thinking History*, London: Routledge, 1995.

18. Lionel Gossman, *Between History and Literature*, Cambridge, MA: Harvard University Press, 1990, p. 286.

19. Hayden White, 'The Historical Text as Literary Artifact', in Robert H. Canary and Henry Kozicki, eds., *The Writing of History: Literary Form and Historical Understanding*, Madison: University of Wisconsin Press, 1978, pp. 42–3.

20. Ibid.

21. Gossman, *Between History and Literature*, p. 288.

22. Edward W. Said, *Culture and Imperialism*, London: Chatto and Windus, 1993, p. 230.

23. Gertrude Himmelfarb, 'Telling It as You Like It', *Times Literary Supplement*, 16 October 1992, p. 14.

24. Said, *Culture and Imperialism*, p. xiii.

25. Edward W. Said, *Orientalism*, London: Penguin, 1978, p. 3.

26. Edward W. Said, 'Foucault and the Imagination of Power', in David Couzens Hoy, ed., *Foucault: A Critical Reader*, Oxford: Blackwell, 1989, p. 149.

27. Michel Foucault, 'Prison Talk', in *Power/Knowledge: Selected Interviews and Other Writings*, ed.

Colin Gordon, Brighton: Harvester Press, 1980, p.51.

28. Ibid.

29. Michel Foucault, *Discipline and Punish: The Birth of the Prison*, trans. Alan Sheridan, New York: Pantheon, 1977, p.27.

30. See Barry Hindess, *Discourses of Power*, Oxford: Basil Blackwell, 1996.

31. Foucault, *Discipline and Punish*, pp.195–228.

32. Michel Foucault, *The Archaeology of Knowledge*, trans. A.M. Sheridan Smith, London: Tavistock, 1972, p.80.

33. Cited in Diane McDonnel, *Theories of Discourse: An Introduction*, Oxford: Basil Blackwell, 1986, p.27.

34. Sara Mills, *Discourse*, London: Routledge, 1997, pp.29–30.

35. John Dunn, 'Crying got Dominion', *Times Literary Supplement*, 16 August 1996, p.28.

36. Foucault, *Discipline and Punish*, p.194.

37. Michel Foucault, *The History of Sexuality*, vol. 1, trans. Robert Hurley, Harmondsworth: Peregrine, 1976, p.10.

38. Raymond Williams, *Politics and Letters: Interview with New Left Review*, London: New Left Books, 1979, p.252.

39. Roger Simon, *Gramsci's Political Thought*, London: Lawrence and Wishart, 1991, p.26.

40. Ibid., p.25.

41. Marx's idea of colonising the Third World for economic development amply indicates the imperialist arrogance geared to the appropriation of primitive society

through domination.

42. See Said, *Orientalism*.

43. Henry Rider Haggard, *King Solomon's Mines*, London: Dent, 1885. See also Denis Riley, 'Am I That Name?' in *Feminism and the Category of 'Women' in History*, Basingstoke: Macmillan, 1989, for a general analysis of gender and racial categories and the essentialisms that have done immense harm to the cause of feminism.

44. Prostitution was a condition of the empire since most of the colonisers were single men. See Anton Gill, *Ruling Passions: Sex, Race and Empire*, London: BBC Books, 1995, pp. 121–41.

45. See Rana Kabbani, *Imperial Fictions: Europe's Myths of Orient*, London: Pandora, 1994, p. 20.

46. Ibid., p. 6.

47. See ibid.

48. Albert Memmi, *The Colonizer and the Colonized* (1957), London: Earthscan, 1990. This classic book is one of the foremost studies of colonial oppression ever written.

49. Gayatri Chakravorty Spivak, *In Other Worlds: Essays in Cultural Politics*. London: Methuen, 1987, p. 109.

50. See Rumina Sethi, *Myths of the Nation: National Identity and Literary Representation,* Oxford: Clarendon, 1999.

51. Edward W. Said, Afterword to *Orientalism*, New York: Vintage, 1994, p. 333.

52. Dennis Porter, 'Orientalism and its Problems', in Francis Barker et al., eds., *The Politics of Theory*, Colchester: University of Essex, 1983, p. 180.

53. Edward W. Said, *The World, the Text, and the Critic*, London: Faber, 1984, p.15.

54. Said, *Culture and Imperialism*, p.xiii.

55. Aijaz Ahmad, *In Theory: Classes, Nations, Literatures*, London: Verso, 1992, p.164.

56. See James Clifford's view in *The Predicament of Culture*, Cambridge, MA: Harvard University Press, 1988, p.263.

57. Said, *Culture and Imperialism*, p.156.

58. Ibid., p.203.

59. Ibid., p.xii.

60. Said, Afterword, p.335.

61. Gyan Prakash, ed., *After Colonialism: Imperial Histories and Postcolonial Displacements*, Princeton, NJ: Princeton University Press, 1995, p.11.

62. Said, Afterword, p.330.

63. Ibid., p.332.

64. Himmelfarb, 'Telling It as You Like It', p.14.

65. Said, *The World, the Text, and the Critic*, p.29.

66. Ibid.

67. Ibid.

68. Ibid., p.35.

69. Ibid., p.6.

70. Said, Afterword, p.331.

71. Ibid.

72. Edward W. Said, *Beginnings: Intentions and Method*, New York: Basic Books, 1974.

73. Said, *The World, the Text, and the Critic*, p.26.

74. Ibid., p.242.

75. Ibid., p.25.

Bibliography

Ahmad, Aijaz, *In Theory: Classes, Nations, Literatures*, London: Verso, 1992.

Ashcroft, Bill, and Ahluwalia, Pal, *Edward Said: The Paradox of Identity*, London: Routledge, 1999.

Clifford, James, *The Predicament of Culture*, Cambridge, MA: Harvard University Press, 1988.

Fanon, Frantz, *The Wretched of the Earth* (1961), trans. Constance Farrington, Harmondsworth: Penguin, 1967.

Foucault, Michel, *Discipline and Punish: The Birth of the Prison*, trans. Alan Sheridan, New York: Pantheon, 1977.

—— *Power/Knowledge: Selected Interviews and Other Writings*, ed. Colin Gordon, Brighton: Harvester Press, 1980.

—— *The Archaeology of Knowledge*, trans. A.M. Sheridan Smith, London: Tavistock, 1972.

—— *The History of Sexuality*, vol. 1, trans. Robert Hurley, Harmondsworth: Peregrine, 1976.

Gill, Anton, *Ruling Passions: Sex, Race and Empire*, London: BBC Books, 1995.

Hindess, Barry, *Discourses of Power*, Oxford: Basil Blackwell, 1996.

Holub, Renate, *Antonio Gramsci: Beyond Marxism and Postmodernism*, London: Routledge, 1992.

Jenkins, Keith, *Re-thinking History*, London: Routledge, 1995.

Kabbani, Rana, *Imperial Fictions: Europe's Myths of Orient*, London: Pandora, 1994.

McDonnel, Diane, *Theories of Discourse: An Introduction*, Oxford: Basil Blackwell, 1986.

Memmi, Albert, *The Colonizer and the Colonized* (1957), London: Earthscan, 1990.

Mills, Sara, *Discourse*, London: Routledge, 1997.

Pearson, Keith Ansell, Parry, Benita, and Squires, Judith, eds., *Cultural Readings of Imperialism: Edward Said and the Gravity of History*, New York: St. Martin's Press, 1997.

Ricoeur, Paul, *History and Truth*, Evanston: Northwestern University Press, 1992.

Rushdie, Salman, *Imaginary Homelands: Essays and Criticism 1981–1991*, London: Granta, 1991.

Said, Edward W., *After the Last Sky*, New York: Pantheon, 1986.

—— Afterword to *Orientalism*, New York: Vintage, 1994.

—— *Beginnings: Intention and Method*, New York: Basic Books, 1975.

—— *Covering Islam*, New York: Vintage, 1981.

—— *Joseph Conrad and the Fiction of Autobiography*, Cambridge, MA: Harvard University Press, 1966.

—— *Culture and Imperialism*, London: Chatto and Windus, 1993.

—— 'Edward Said', interview with Imre Salusinszky, *Criticism in Society*, London: Methuen, 1987, pp. 123–48.

—— 'Orientalism Reconsidered', in Barker, Francis, et al., *Europe and Its Others*, vol. 1, Colchester: University of Essex, 1985, pp. 14–27.

—— 'Reflections of an Exile', interview with Nikhil Padgaonkar, *Biblio*, vol. 4, Nov–Dec 1999, p. 13.

—— 'Foucault and the Imagination of Power', in David Couzens Hoy, ed., *Foucault: A Critical Reader*, Oxford: Blackwell, 1989.

—— *Orientalism*, London: Penguin, 1978.

—— *Out of Place*, London: Granta, 2000.

—— *Peace and its Discontents*, New York: Vintage, 1995.

—— 'Representations of the Intellectual' (Reith Lectures), *The Independent*, 24 June; 1 July; 8 July; 15 July; 22 July; 29 July; 1993.

—— *The Politics of Dispossession*, London: Chatto and Windus, 1994.

—— *The Question of Palestine*, London: Vintage, 1980.

—— *The World, the Text, and the Critic*, London: Faber, 1984.

Sethi, Rumina, *Myths of the Nation: National Identity and Literary Representation*, Oxford: Clarendon, 1999.

Simon, Roger, *Gramsci's Political Thought*, London: Lawrence and Wishart, 1991.

Spivak, Gayatri Chakravorty, *In Other Worlds: Essays in Cultural Politics*, London: Methuen, 1987.

Sprinker, Michael, *Edward Said: A Critical Reader*, Oxford: Blackwell, 1992.

White, Hayden, *Metahistory: The Historical Imagination in Nineteenth-Century Europe*, Baltimore: Johns Hopkins University Press, 1973.

—— *The Content and the Form: Narrative Discourse and Historical Representation*, Baltimore: Johns Hopkins University Press, 1987.

Williams, Raymond, *Politics and Letters: Interviews with New Left Review*, London: New Left Review, 1979.

—— *Problems in Materialism and Culture: Selected Essays*, London: Verso, 1980.

Key Ideas

Canon

A well-preserved body of books, practices and attitudes by which 'truth' is presented to the rest of the world. The word 'canon' underscores the existence of a powerful group that creates 'classics' through the principle of an arbitrary exclusion and inclusion. F.R. Leavis's selection of a group of writers who constitute the 'Great Tradition' is an example. The Shakespeare industry is another. The existing canon is now being continuously overwhelmed by World Literature and Popular Culture, thus ending the cultural myopia of the eurocentric curriculum and shifting the focus of literary study from the canonical to Cultural Studies.

Colonialism

The practice of constructing settlements or colonies in imperial territories with the purpose of establishing trade and production. Colonialism establishes a political order and an administration to run successfully. Domination is imposed either by force or hegemony, or both. Colonialism is accompanied by exploitation, annexation and conquest. Its hegemonic power rests on creating the binary oppositions of self/other, white/black, good/evil, superior/inferior, and so on. Thus a part of the world was able to enjoy supremacy because it convinced the rest of the world about the 'white man's burden' and his 'civilising mission'.

Discourse

Any speech, writing or belief through which the world can

be known and understood. In the Foucauldian sense, discourse contains statements which are governed by unspoken rules yielding a language of power co-ordinated through knowledge. We can say that there is no 'truth', and that all knowledge is a 'will to power'. A determining and defining authority is created through the power of discourse which has the underpinnings of cultural imperialism.

Hegemony

In attempting to see how the ruling class successfully promotes its ideology, Antonio Gramsci, an Italian Marxist, spoke of a rule of power in which the very thought of the colonised is controlled to secure consent. The term may be usefully applied to imperial practice which manifests itself in two ways: through direct domination and through invoking consent. The latter is hegemonic. Hegemony, from the perspective of imperial rule, implies the use of strategic manoeuvres that imperceptibly influence the natives to believe that eurocentric assumptions are quite naturally superior to their own. Hegemony smacks only of repressive myths to which society collectively gives its consent. It consists of the ideas of the ruling material forces of society.

Imperialism

The domination over territories not your own constitutes imperialism. Imperialism is associated with European countries like Britain, France, Holland, Portugal, Spain and Belgium which formed empires in Asia, Africa and Latin America for economic and political interest.

Master narrative

The term is synonymous with 'grand narrative', which Jean-François Lyotard uses in his book *The Postmodern Condition*. Such narratives are based on transcendental truths and signify ideological systems such as the Enlightenment, eurocentrism, Christianity or Hinduism. Such authoritarian and totalising universalisms now stand discredited in the face of the local or the 'periphery'. For instance, it is being argued more and more that eurocentrism represents a universal value-free point of view which empowers the History of Europe as the master narrative or hegemonic discourse that takes the histories of South Asia or Africa as subordinate variations on it.

Postcolonial

Although implying a historical rupture signifying the end of the colonial chapter, 'postcolonial' means much more. It covers all writing related to colonial experience with the exclusion of the colonising powers themselves. This writing has a revisionist focus and questions the liberal-humanist conceptions of Enlightenment thought.

Subaltern

Subaltern literally means 'of lower rank'. The word assumes especial importance in the exercise of self-representation with the intention of undermining existing master narratives. This subversive effort would bring the margins to the centre and produce subaltern history which is usually ignored in élite writing and interpretation.